~~“I fee~~l hope pouring in the rain.
Being myself is enough.”

—DARA MCANULTY

“My body is actually me.
And it’s not out to get me.”

—BILLIE EILISH

“Words matter. How we talk
about disabilities matters deeply.”

—HELENA DONATO-SAPP

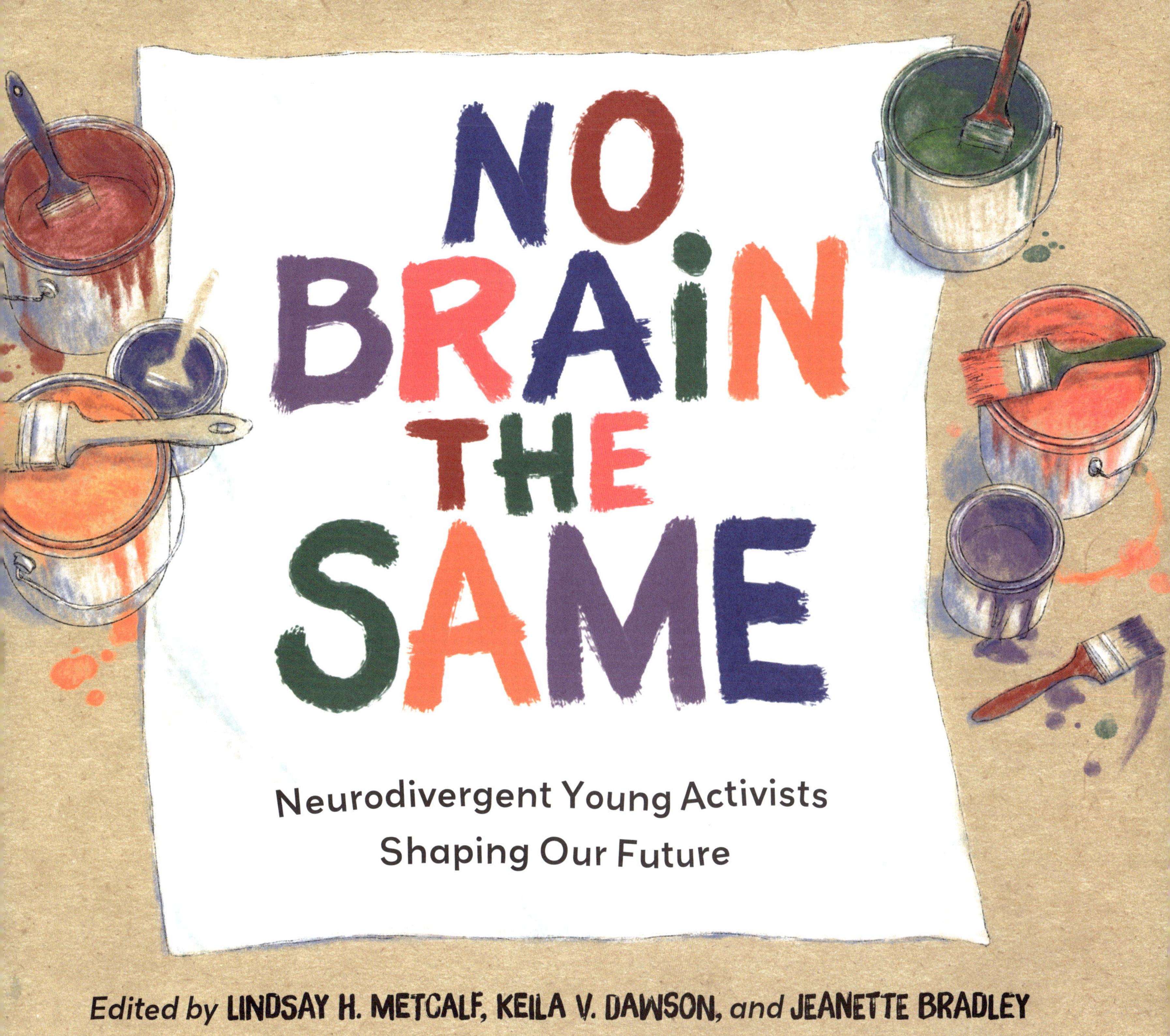

No Brain the Same

Neurodivergent Young Activists Shaping Our Future

Edited by LINDSAY H. METCALF, KEILA V. DAWSON, *and* JEANETTE BRADLEY

Illustrated by JEANETTE BRADLEY

Charlesbridge

WE ARE THE FUTURE

A kenning poem by Jeanette Bradley

We are the open dreamers,
the deep feelers,
the big thinkers,
the magic makers.

We are the truth speakers,
the heart singers,
the peace fighters,
the justice leaders.

We are the fierce self-lovers,
the laughing healers,
the bond builders,
the hope bringers.

We are the path pavers,
the leap takers,
the quest seekers,
the system changers.

We are the extra. The ordinary.
We are the future.
Extraordinary.

In this book you will meet fourteen neurodivergent young activists who are trailblazing for themselves, for their communities, and for our planet. Each activist inspired a poet who shares an aspect of their identity. Look for tips on ways you can use your talents and passions to work for change and check the glossary at the end for unfamiliar words. **BELIEVE** in yourself, **REACH** out to others, and **LEAD**!

CONNOR DEWOLFE: *WHAT IF . . .*

A free-verse poem by e.E. Charlton-Trujillo

Imagine:
Worldwide lockdown.
Home stuck.
Zoom school.

Now imagine a mind:
Swarmed with racing thoughts—intrusive thoughts,
unexpected tears, time disappeared,
anxiety, can't sleep, forgot to eat—
Different—not wrong—neurodivergent. ADHD—
hyperfocused, excited, bored, creative,
fidgety, overwhelmed—

THEN . . .

What if other people feel like me?

Alone.
In a sea of bees.

Now imagine after:
Six months of TikTok posts
when *ADHD Superpowers* explodes—goes viral!
Over five million people soon follow
this extraordinary mind
that sparked accidental genius:

Other people feel like me.

Connor DeWolfe makes funny TikToks about managing his attention-deficit/hyperactivity disorder (ADHD) in his personal life and professional acting career. Connor's videos describe how his attention, behavior, and emotions can sometimes be too much or too little, inspiring others to seek diagnosis and feel less alone. He breaks down terms like *intrusive thoughts*, *dopamine*, *info-dumping*, and *sensory processing* while offering ADHD life hacks to his followers.

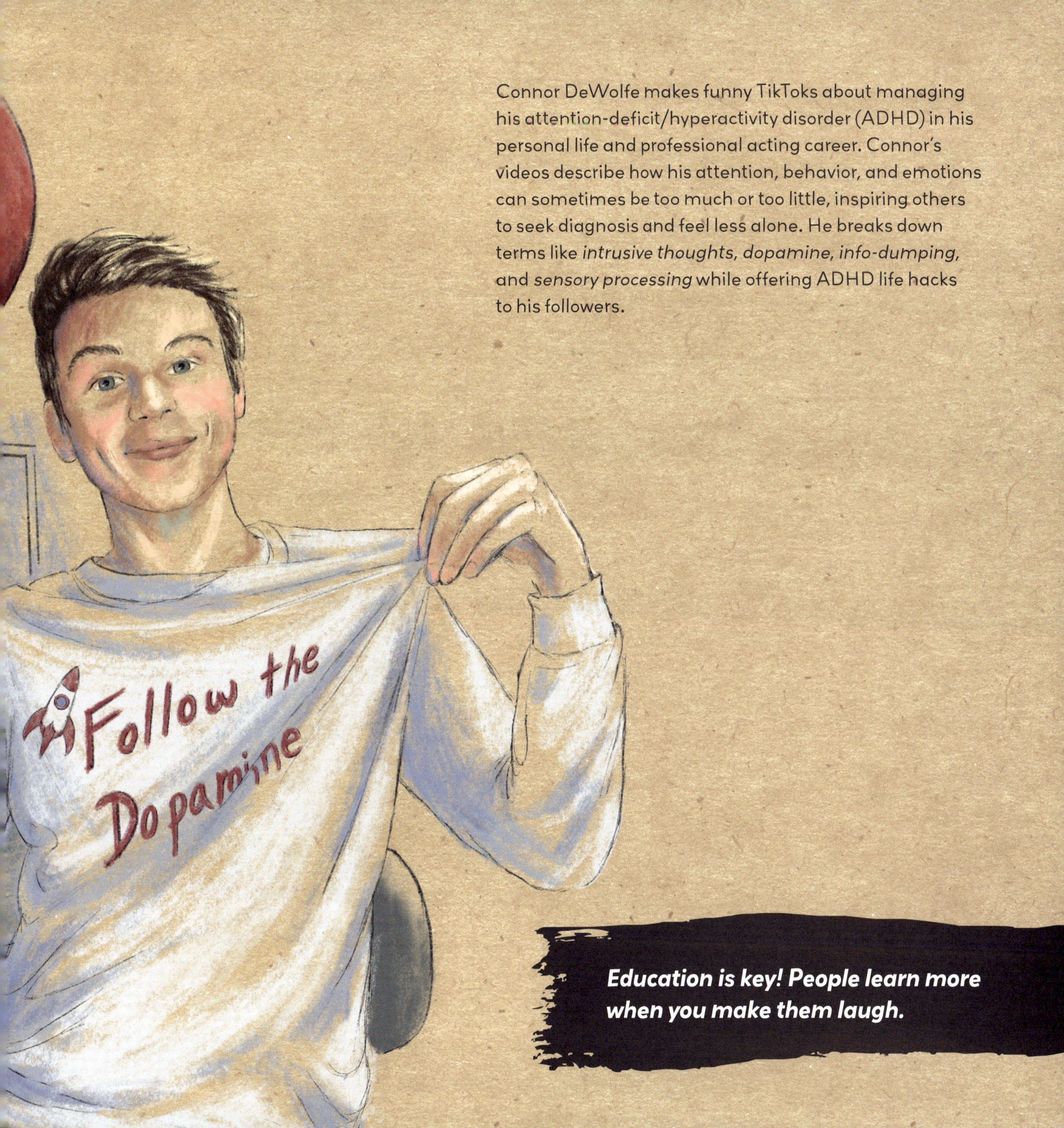

Education is key! People learn more when you make them laugh.

HELENA DONATO-SAPP: *HER NAME MEANS LIGHT*

A double couplet series by **Vanessa Brantley-Newton**

Among all the minds, a beacon shines bright.
Look for Helena, a star in the night.
This poet and activist makes her voice heard.
In the chorus of change, she sings every word.

She's young yet wise beyond her years.
Facing adversity, she conquers her fears.
Learning disabled? Some see a flaw.
She sees a strength, leaving others in awe.

Helena the poet weaves a pure tale
of resilience and hope. She sets her sail.
In the sea of diversity, she finds her place—
a beacon of change for the vast human race.

Born in a world that's quick to define,
Helena enlightens, line after line.
A Black girl. A force. A true inspiration.
A call for acceptance. A standing ovation!

Navigating school with a visual processing disorder, a memory disorder, dyscalculia, and ADHD, Helena Donato-Sapp experienced bullying from classmates and a lack of support from adults. But instead of accepting a negative view of herself, Helena became a speaker and writer who advocates for disabled kids to craft "an armor of self-worth." In middle school Helena received standing ovations when speaking at conferences for teachers and librarians. "My work is about refusing shame for any of my identities," she says.

Take pride in the unique way you learn. Ask for what you need to succeed academically.

BILLIE EILISH: *LIGHTNING*

A free-verse poem by Devin Murphy

A girl with Tourette's
learned to write songs with a lightning bolt
Turned extra electricity into brilliance
twisted tics into chords
a twitch to perfect pitch
What could not be contained
she contained in a lyric

Let it out

She saw through ocean eyes
and rode sound waves to fame
Learned to fly with wings once stuck in mud
An inner calm with a lack of control
left her soul in notes
when hope was too brittle to hold

Let Billie show you how to take pride
in what you might want to hide
And face each day brimming with all you can be

Let it out

like Billie

Beyond winning nine Grammy Awards and two Oscars by age twenty-two, Billie Eilish uses her pop-star platform to fight climate change. She inspires concertgoers to eat a plant-based diet, refill water bottles, rock recycled fashion, and vote. Cameras sometimes capture Billie's sudden movements, called tics. Suppressing them can be painful, and she won't let them stop her. Billie has become a role model for neurodivergent youth since opening up about living with Tourette's syndrome, depression, synesthesia, and hypermobility.

Celebrate all parts of you. By being open, you help yourself while giving others courage to do the same.

DARA MCANULTY: *WILD CHILD*

A free-verse poem by Sally J. Pla

Dara's Wilderness:

Raptors wheeling through the sky.
The dappled shade of an ancient oak.
Tadpoles frothing the edge of a pond.
Moss so green it seems to glow.

Dara's Bewilderness:

Flickering lights in a noisy schoolroom.
Screeching bells and crowded halls.
Evil taunts from playground bullies.
Never knowing what to say . . .

What soothes, salves, and saves us
is Wilderness.
And Dara knows this well:
He loves and advocates for Nature,
speaks heart-deep for it
everywhere he goes.

The wild is Dara's refuge,
but not just his:
We are all Wild Children.
And saving Nature
is the only way
we can save
ourselves.

Dara McAnulty calls nature "medicine for this overactive brain." At thirteen Dara began blogging about the plants and animals he encountered at home in Ireland. His rich, joyful descriptions were published as *Diary of a Young Naturalist*, which won two national book awards in the United Kingdom. The autistic teen, whose name means "oak" in Irish, was once taunted for talking too much about the environment. But he persisted, shared his passion with crowds of up to ten thousand people, and received honors from the British prime minister.

Keep a journal to process your deep feelings.

SADIE McCALLUM: *SADIE REINVENTS THE WHEEL*

A tercet series by Liv Mammone

A girl saw a curb, saw a wheel, saw a door.
Saw herself, the library, the sea.
Sadie saw everywhere she wanted to be.

Wheels spun in her mind and next to her feet.
They spun in her dreams.
Sadie dreamed—and she drew.

With the help of her family, she built something new.
Inventing wheels that could push and rise,
she saw her walker with an inventor's eyes.

This machine that helped her move so much
now had wheels made of tougher stuff
to conquer concrete curbs!

This girl saw a door. A way up. Saw herself
climbing higher, stepping toward
a more inclusive future.

Sadie McCallum has cerebral palsy, and she's good at building things. Navigating physical barriers isn't easy for Sadie, so at age nine, she and her younger sister, Claire, invented a multi-wheeled walker that climbs over curbs and steps. Since appearing on *The Tonight Show Starring Jimmy Fallon* with the Amazing Curb Climber, Sadie has won many regional and national invention competitions and advised engineers who make mobility equipment. Sadie's physical challenges drive her creative spirit and innovation.

Use your unique perspective to solve problems.

ADAM WOLFOND: *DEAR ADAM*

A free-verse poem by Hannah Emerson

Make freedom free
greeting dreamer dreaming freedom
dreaming reality reality

dear reality reality
freeing everyone
dreaming freedom.

Growing reality dreaming reality
becoming reality yearning reality
greeting reality reality reality reality reality

becoming freedom greeting
dear dear dear Adam
yes yes yes yes.

Look reality so close
greeting freedom
yearning becoming reality

dreaming dreaming
becoming water reality
helping dear dear dear great dreamer

floating reality
becoming dear great treeing
named Adam yes yes.

Adam Wolfond is a nonspeaking autistic poet who communicates through typing and movement, often with a stick. At fourteen, Adam cofounded a community of neurodivergent artists called dis assembly. He published his first chapbook of poetry at seventeen. Adam creates art installations about his lived experience with neurodivergent language, which he calls "languaging the ways of water." He completed his master's degree at a Canadian university and continues to speak publicly using a text-to-speech app.

Write a poem, make art, or use movement to communicate your message.

LIAM GARNER: *NO JOURNEY TOO LONG*

A free-verse poem by Jen Malia

The Pan-American Highway.
Alaska to Argentina.
Fourteen countries.
20,000 miles.
When you're on the bike, Liam says,
you're forced to go through these undiscovered places.

No challenge too big.
Not 100-degree days in the jungle of southern Mexico.
Not blacking out after hitting a pothole in Colombia.
Forty stitches and back on the road.
I knew no matter what happened,
Liam says,
even if I lost an arm,
I was still doing it.

No journey too long.
527 days on the road.
He believed in himself.
And made it to the finish line.

Don't put off your dreams.

Just make a step-by-step list, Liam says,

and do the first step.

Liam Garner felt stifled in school. On his bike, he was free. After graduation, a wild idea hit him: What if he biked from the top of the world to the bottom? "I would never be able to doubt myself again." The autistic Mexican American teen pushed off from Prudhoe Bay, Alaska, and reached Ushuaia, Argentina, a year and a half later. On TikTok, the view from above his handlebars showcased Earth's majestic beauty—trickling waterfalls, lunarlike deserts, aquamarine glaciers—while the roadblocks of youth, culture, borders, and self-doubt rolled away.

Break down big goals into small tasks.

LY XĪNZHÈN M. ZHǍNGSŪN BROWN: *THE DEEPEST FEELING*

A free-verse poem by A. J. Sass

I may not show it
in a way people can see,
yet I feel deeply.

This makes me want to help
whenever I see injustice
within my community.

My skin prickled at the thought
of kids like me receiving
electric shocks
in school.

It was a thousand kicks to my gut
whenever police treated people
like they deserved to be punished
just for being autistic.

I couldn't stay quiet.
Couldn't look away
or turn off my empathy.

I worked to change harmful school policies.
I educated those in positions of authority.

Because autistic folks deserve safety and respect,
just as much as anyone.

At fifteen, Ly Xīnzhèn M. Zhǎngsūn Brown worked with their state senator to introduce a bill that would require Massachusetts police officers to learn about autism and developmental disabilities. As part of the Autistic Self-Advocacy Network, Ly Xīnzhèn testified against the use of electric shocks to punish autistic students at a school and residential center for kids and adults. Ly Xīnzhèn's activism grew during college and law school, and they continue to seek justice for autistic people of color.

If you witness or experience bullying or violence, reach out to a trusted adult. Keep communicating until you see change.

JAZMINE WILDCAT: MENDING HEARTS, RAISING VOICES

An American sonnet by CooXooEii Black

Nii'iini: *"Things are good."*

In the heart of the Wind River's warm embrace,
it was good when a second grader raised her voice
and a cardboard banner above her head.
It was good when she shouted down domestic violence.

She began mending hearts bruised by the night,
but even the best of us struggle in our minds.
Depression and anxiety struck like an angry snake,
but it was good when Jazmine's voice rose again to seek help.

Her community listened and wrapped her in love.
Despite mental struggles, her courage grew,
and she crafted a legacy of breaking down walls.
It was good when she got involved in mental health talk.

Her compassion is a balm for her people's troubled hours.
It is good that she helps minds to flourish and embrace their power.

In second grade, Jazmine Wildcat rallied to support protections for Native women in the federal Violence Against Women Act. The Northern Arapaho citizen grew up watching her mother and grandmother volunteer at a local domestic violence shelter on the Wind River Reservation in Wyoming. Activism carried Jazmine through her teenage depression and anxiety, even when she couldn't find a therapist who understood her culture. She created the Nii'iini Project to heal intergenerational trauma through volunteerism and activism. Jazmine wants to work in national health policy and administration someday.

Work with friends for social change and heal yourself in the process.

ANDY SMITH: *AVATAR*

A concrete poem by Lyn Miller-Lachmann

No one listens
when we tell adults
about the kids
who pick
on us in
school.
Except for this online place
created by someone like us.
His name is Andy,
and he was picked
on all the time
in school
because he's different. Autistic.
We play games like *Minecraft*,
our favorite.
Make friends,
kids like us.
Andy listens.
He helps
us to tell our stories.

Andy Smith believed fitting in would make him happy, but masking his differences drained his energy. The strong student became so tired at university that he couldn't leave his room and failed his exams. Questioning his existence, he posted on social media and connected with a community of autistic people who understood. Fostering that same fellowship for young people became his mission. Andy's nonprofit, Spectrum Gaming, gathers neurodivergent youth in the UK through games like *Minecraft*, online chats, in-person forest school, and autism-acceptance courses for those who want to learn more.

Create a club around shared interests to support yourself and others.

MOLLY SEIDEL: *THE LONGEST RACE*

A collage poem with italicized quotations by Jeanette Bradley

Running a marathon means going
hard for 26.2 miles. 55,000 steps after steps.
You don't block out the pain, you say:
I feel this, and I'm going
to keep going anyway.

I don't know why my brain just can't work

the way other people's brains work. Why it goes
100 miles per hour, *but when I'm running*
my mind fits into my body. Everything
just makes sense. Keep going, keep going.

How many steps to loving yourself? *I'm always going*
to have to work at this, and it's always going
to be hard. You don't have to be perfect.
Keep going, keep going, keep going anyway.

The longest race is toward joy.
Nothing bad stays bad forever.
You just. Got to.
Keep. Going.

In high school and college, Molly Seidel won race after race, but privately she struggled with obsessive compulsive disorder (OCD), disordered eating, and undiagnosed ADHD. Molly began to prioritize her mental health and changed her approach to running after her poor nutrition weakened her bones to the breaking point. She ran her first-ever marathon at the 2020 US Olympic trials and went on to win the bronze medal in Tokyo. Molly continues to use her platform to promote active self-care for mental health.

Sharing your struggles helps you and shows others they are not alone.

MIA ARMSTRONG: *WORDS UNSPOKEN*

A free-verse poem by Fiona Morris

No voice is unspoken,
I say to the waves, even though my thoughts
tell me otherwise.

I turn off all that noise from the crowd.
Now everyone will hear me out,
my heart speaking louder than their words.

I keep on climbing till I reach the top.
Every time I fall, I just get back up again.
I will be stronger than anything
that stands in my way.

I breathe in and out, the summer air.
I say the words unspoken.
At sunset my hands leave prints
on the beach, telling you I was here.

Mia Armstrong is an actress, activist, author, and adventurer. She has appeared in movies and shows for Netflix, Apple TV, and Disney. Mia loves physical challenges, so activities like surfing and rock climbing help with her low muscle tone. Today she speaks about living with Down syndrome in "One Minute with Mia" Instagram videos. She says she wrote the picture book *I Am a Masterpiece!* "to inspire other people to love their own stories and be proud of who they are."

Representation matters. When others see you doing what you love, they know they belong, too.

MOLLIE DAVIS: *WHAT LOVE SOUNDS LIKE*

A free-verse poem by Jordan Scott

I can speak louder than a gunshot.
I promise you.
Sometimes it may seem like my words are stuck.
Like all the sounds of the world
shiver and shake on my lips.
But that's just me.
Talking like the wind, rivers,
goldfinches, and whales.
I know all the sounds for crying and heartbreak.
But I also know what love sounds like.
It's children coming home from school.
I know so many words.
More than the stars at night.
I can say them all, beautifully and bright.
I can speak louder than a gunshot.
I promise.
You can too.

Mollie Davis has practiced lockdown drills since kindergarten. When she survived a shooting at her Maryland high school and her schoolmate did not, Mollie knew she must speak out. She took the mic at a national rally and unfurled a forty-page list of school shootings in the US. People left rude comments online about her stuttering, and her television interview never aired. But she hasn't stopped talking: Mollie went to law school because she refuses to stay silent.

Your voice matters. It's more important to speak up than to speak perfectly.

CILLIAN O'CONNOR: *CILLIAN'S MAGIC*

A free-verse poem by K. A. Reynolds

When I was younger,
others could make my words
        vanish
just by walking into a room,

and the only trick I knew
was
how to
        disappear.

I felt incomplete.
Empty.
Invisible
        to the world.

But the moment I found magic,
it was like
all the lights in the universe
flashed on.

And suddenly
I
was
found.

Every word and joy
and wonder
trapped inside me
grew wings   and   flew.

And all at once
I knew
how to connect
to the world.

Magic showed me that anything is possible
if you truly believe. And I truly believe
your big dreams
will find you, too.

Cillian O'Connor is an award-winning magician who loves to make people smile. While he sometimes struggles with conversation, this autistic teen says, "I let the magic speak for me." Performing magic also helps Cillian with his dyspraxia by strengthening weak muscles in his hands. He became the youngest member of the Society of Irish Magicians at age eight and has since competed on *Britain's Got Talent*, placing third, and *America's Got Talent*. Cillian wants to inspire other neurodivergent youth to find their own magic.

Share something you're good at with others. Invite them to see the whole you.

CROSSROADS

A pair of nonets by Lindsay H. Metcalf

Your brain is a road map. Neurons fire,
growing roads, sometimes straight, sometimes
twisty. Sometimes roadblocks look
like dead ends, but if you
keep navigating,
a path evolves.
The map is
yours to
draw.

You
may zig
while others
zag. If their trails
differ from yours, so
what? Trust that connections
exist. Seek them and unite
to clear a passage to justice.
Believe: together we'll heal the world.

Consider . . .

What do you care about? What are you good at?
What do you need to overcome or change?
Who else cares?
What rights do you have?
What brings you joy? What empowers you?

WHERE TO BEGIN?

Like the people in this book, you may begin your activism journey with self-love. **BELIEVE** in yourself and your power. **REACH** out and connect with people who share your passions. Then use your unique strengths to **LEAD** all kinds of minds!

Believe

You have value. Mia knows we are all masterpieces just the way we are.
You are not broken. Helena refuses shame for her identities.
You are not invisible. Cillian found his magical place in the world.
You are capable of incredible things. Liam works to achieve his goals.

Reach

It's OK if you're not OK. Molly took the brave step of asking for help.
You are not alone. Andy found a supportive autistic community online.
You can find joy. Connor connects people through laughter.
You can solve big problems with others. Billie rallies fans around climate change.

Lead

You can speak out. Mollie knows she has important things to say.
Your words matter. Dara inspires through his writing.
Your experiences matter. Sadie's physical challenges inform her inventions.
You can shape your own path. Adam combines his creativity with community.
You can heal by taking action. Jazmine advocates, which helps her and others.
You have the power to make change. Ly Xīnzhèn connects people and changes policies.

SHINE

A diamante poem by Keila V. Dawson

Believe:
Worthy, worthwhile.
Wanting, hoping, thinking.
Be the someone—**reach**—who does something.
Connecting, building, upstanding.
Bold. Fearless.
Lead!

GLOSSARY

ableism/ableist: Favoring able-bodied, neurotypical people in an individual or systemic way. See also: *neurotypical*.

ADHD (attention-deficit/hyperactivity disorder): A brain-based disorder that may affect executive function, sensory processing, movement, and communication. See also: *executive function* and *sensory processing disorder*.

anxiety disorder: Persistent feelings of worry or dread that interfere with daily life and can affect physical health.

autism: A brain-based disability that may affect executive function, thinking, sensory processing, movement, and social communication. *Note: This book uses the adjective "autistic" because many autistic people feel that identity-first language reflects pride in this fundamental part of their identity.*

cerebral palsy: A brain disorder that affects a person's ability to control muscles and movement.

depression: Long-lasting feelings of sadness, low energy, and trouble concentrating that interfere with daily life.

disability/disabled: A mental or physical condition that affects a person's ability to function in daily life. The supports and accommodations available in a community or country affect the personal experience of being disabled.

disordered eating: Unhealthy behaviors related to food and eating that can cause physical harm to a person's body.

domestic violence: Violence among people who live together.

dopamine: A chemical messenger made in the brain that makes a person feel good.

Down syndrome: A chromosomal disorder in which a person has forty-seven chromosomes instead of the expected forty-six. This may affect thinking, hearing, speech, and physical development.

dyscalculia: A learning disability that affects a person's ability to understand numbers and math.

dyslexia: A learning disability that affects a person's ability to read, spell, and write.

dyspraxia: A brain-based disorder that affects a person's ability to plan and coordinate movement.

executive function: A person's ability to make plans, focus on tasks, and control or coordinate thoughts and actions.

hypermobility: Very flexible joints that can cause pain or injury.

info-dumping: Talking for a long time about something without being sure the listener is interested.

intrusive thoughts: Unwanted thoughts that a person can't control well.

masking: Hiding natural neurodivergent behaviors and mirroring neurotypical behaviors to avoid harm. See also: *neurodivergent* and *neurotypical*.

neurodivergent: A word to describe people whose brains are structured differently or work differently from an average person's brain; may be labeled as a disability in an ableist society. See also: *ableism*.

neurons: Nerve cells throughout the body that communicate messages between the brain and muscles.

neurotypical: A word to describe people whose brains have the structure that's considered the norm by their society.

nonspeaking: A word to describe a person who may write, type, or use an assistive device to communicate rather than using spoken language.

mobility: The ability to move.

OCD (obsessive-compulsive disorder): A brain difference that causes intrusive thoughts and behaviors that a person repeats over and over to relieve upsetting feelings.

sensory processing disorder: When a person's brain has trouble understanding information received through the senses. See also: *visual processing disorder*.

stuttering: A brain-based disorder that causes repetitions of sounds or pauses when speaking.

synesthesia: When information the brain receives stimulates more than one sense at a time.

tic: An uncontrollable sudden movement or vocal sound that can be recurring.

Tourette's syndrome: A brain-related condition that causes tics.

trauma: The emotional impact of living through an upsetting event.

visual processing disorder: When a person's brain has trouble making sense of information received through sight.

POETRY FORMS

American sonnet: A fourteen-line poem without the rhyme and meter constraints of a traditional sonnet.

collage poem: A type of found poem that includes words, phrases, or quotations from other sources, combined with the poet's own words.

concrete poem: A poem shaped like its topic that can fill in or outline a shape.

diamante: A poem made up of seven lines shaped like a diamond. The first and last lines have one word, the second and sixth lines have two adjectives, the fourth line has nouns or a short phrase, and the third and fourth lines have *-ing* words.

double couplets: Four-lined stanzas (quatrains) composed of two rhyming pairs.

free-verse poem: This unrestricted style does not need to rhyme or follow a beat pattern.

kenning poem: A poem that uses invented two-word descriptions in place of familiar nouns. Originally from Old Norse and Old English traditions.

nonet: A nine-line poem with nine syllables in the first line, eight syllables in the next line, seven in the next, and so on, with one syllable in the final line (or the reverse).

tercet: A stanza, or set, of three lines.

ABOUT THE POETS

CooXooEii Black (he/him) is an Afro-Indigenous poet from the Wind River Reservation and a member of the Northern Arapaho Tribe. He is the author of *The Morning You Saw a Train of Stars Streaking Across the Sky*. His work is deeply rooted in his heritage and oral tradition, exploring childhood memories, Reservation life, land, and faith.

Jeanette Bradley (she/her) uses her ADHD-fueled creativity and hyperfocus to write, draw, and make books for kids. She coedited and illustrated *No Voice Too Small* and *No World Too Big*, companion titles to *No Brain the Same*, and is the author/illustrator of other picture books. Jeanette lives in Rhode Island with her wife and kids. **jeanettebradley.com**

Vanessa Brantley-Newton (she/her) is the author and illustrator of *Grandma's Purse* and *Just Like Me* and has illustrated many children's books. She studied fashion illustration at the Fashion Institute of Technology and children's book illustration at the School of Visual Arts in New York. Vanessa is dyslexic and has synesthesia. She makes her nest in Charlotte, North Carolina. **vanessabrantleynewton.com**

e.E. Charlton-Trujillo (they/them) is a Mexican American filmmaker and author of many celebrated books for children and young adults, including the American Library Association award-winning Fat Angie series. e.E. cofounded the nonprofit Never Counted Out, which empowers youth literacy. e.E. has ADHD. **eecharlton-trujillo.com**

Keila V. Dawson (she/her) has worked in schools and clinical settings in the United States and abroad as an educator and advocate for children with a wide range of disabilities. She is a coeditor of *No Voice Too Small* and *No World Too Big*, companion titles to *No Brain the Same*, and the author of other nonfiction and fiction books. **keiladawson.com**

Hannah Emerson (she/her) is the author of *The Kissing of Kissing* and *You Are Helping This Great Universe Explode*. She is a nonspeaking autistic poet whose work has appeared in many publications, as well as her Substack, *The Kissing Nothing We Become*. She lives in Lafayette, New York. **hannah-emerson.com**

Jen Malia (she/her) is the author of The Infinity Rainbow Club chapter book series and *Too Sticky! Sensory Issues with Autism*. She is a professor of English and the creative writing coordinator at Norfolk State University. She has a PhD in English from the University of Southern California. Jen is autistic and an explorer. **jenmalia.com**

Liv Mammone (she/her) is an editor and poet from Long Island. In 2017, she was the first disabled woman on a New York national poetry slam team. A Brooklyn Poets fellow and Zoeglossia fellow, she is an editor at Game Over Books. Her first poetry collection was published in 2025. **livmammonepoems.com**

Lindsay H. Metcalf (she/her) is a former journalist and author of nonfiction and poetry for children. She is a coeditor of the poetry anthologies *No Voice Too Small* and *No World Too Big*, companion titles to *No Brain the Same*. She lives with her neurodiverse family in north-central Kansas, a few miles from the family farm where she grew up. **lindsayhmetcalf.com**

Lyn Miller-Lachmann (she/her) is the author of a Temple Grandin biography, a picture book, and multiple novels featuring autistic characters like her. Her novel *Torch* won the Los Angeles Times Book Prize for YA literature. Lyn has constructed a giant Lego town, which she considers a *Minecraft*-adjacent activity. **lynmillerlachmann.com**

Fiona Morris (she/her) doesn't let Down syndrome define her. Passionate about writing since she could first hold a pencil, Fiona is the author of a book of original poems, *Poetry Tingles the Heart*. Her work has been featured in several collections and publications.

Devin Murphy (he/him) is a former teen slam poetry champion and was featured on HBO's *Brave New Voices*. He was diagnosed with Tourette's syndrome at age ten. He attended the University of California, Berkeley for his undergraduate studies and holds a master's degree in cultural anthropology from the University of Hawai'i. Devin lives on O'ahu and runs a small organic farm.

Sally J. Pla (she/her) is the award-winning author of books including *The Someday Birds* and cofounder of anovelmind.com, which explores neurodiversity and mental health in children's literature. She believes in the beauty of different brains and in stories where different kids can see themselves, sometimes for the first time. She's autistic. **sallyjpla.com**

K. A. Reynolds (she/her) is an autistic poet, autism and mental health advocate, and the author of several books, including *Izzy at the End of the World* and *The Big Worry Day*. She uses her voice, hope, and magic to show what amazing things big dreamers can do. **kareynoldsbooks.com**

A. J. Sass (he/they) is a critically acclaimed and award-winning author of books for children and teen readers. Originally from the Midwest, he currently lives in the San Francisco Bay Area with his husband. A. J. aims to educate, foster empathy, and spread awareness by writing and speaking about the autistic experience. **sassinsf.com**

Jordan Scott (he/him) is a poet and children's author. His debut children's book, *I Talk Like a River*, won the Schneider Family Book Award for artistic expression of the disability experience. Jordan also received the Latner Griffin Writers' Trust Poetry Prize for mid-career poets. He teaches children's literature at the University of British Columbia. **jordanscottwrites.com**

For my extraordinary young models: Adam, Anders, Ariadne, Beatrice, Emmi, Maddie, and Nate. Shine on!—J. B.

To all the youth who refuse to stay silent.—K. V. D.

For Will, Quinn, and Bennett, whose brains I love most.—L. H. M.

Charlesbridge • 9 Galen Street, Watertown, MA 02472
www.charlesbridge.com

Library of Congress Cataloging-in-Publication Data
Names: Metcalf, Lindsay H. editor | Dawson, Keila V. editor | Bradley, Jeanette editor, illustrator
Title: No brain the same: neurodivergent young activists shaping our future / edited by Lindsay H. Metcalf, Keila V. Dawson, and Jeanette Bradley; illustrated by Jeanette Bradley.
Description: Watertown, MA: Charlesbridge, 2026. | Audience: Ages 5–9 | Audience: Grades 2–3 | Summary: "Vanessa Brantley-Newton, e.E. Charlton-Trujillo, and others present poems about neurodivergent activists who have made changes in their community and in the world."—Provided by publisher.
Identifiers: LCCN 2025012024 (print) | LCCN 2025012025 (ebook) | ISBN 9781623545833 hardcover | ISBN 9781632894540 ebook
Subjects: LCSH: Social justice—Juvenile poetry | Social action—Juvenile poetry | Neurodivergent people—Juvenile poetry | Children's poetry, American | CYAC: Social justice—Poetry | Social action—Poetry | Neurodivergent people—Poetry | American poetry | LCGFT: Poetry
Classification: LCC PS595.S75 N59 2026 (print) | LCC PS595.S75 (ebook)
LC record available at https://lccn.loc.gov/2025012024
LC ebook record available at https://lccn.loc.gov/2025012025

Printed in China • OPIC
The authorized representative in the EU for product safety and compliance is eucomply OÜPärnu mnt 139b-14, 11317 Tallinn, Estonia, hello@eucompliancepartner.com, +33757690241
(hc) 10 9 8 7 6 5 4 3 2 1

Illustrations painted digitally in Procreate for iPad on a digital paper designed by Paper Farms
Text type set in Grenadine MVB by Markanna Studios Inc.
Edited by Karen Boss
Designed by Diane M. Earley
Production supervised by Nicole Turner

"I have a purpose, just like you."

—MIA ARMSTRONG

"The only way I can be happy and thrive is to stop trying to fit in."

—ANDY SMITH

"Change happens when we change one person's perspective."

—MOLLIE DAVIS